CW00385752

ANOTHER SON OF YORKSHIRE

A true, moving and informative
story of a lad born on the
Yorkshire Moors.

To Marie,

Without your words
this book may never
have been by writer.

KATHLEEN SYLVIA CLARK

Kathleen Sylvia Clark.

9/5/1996.

ISBN 1 872239 12 9

INTRODUCTION

My father will be ninety in 1995. For many years he has entertained his family, friends and acquaintances with stories of his early life in the farming communities of North Yorkshire. An unwillingness to let these tales die inspired me to put pen to paper.

Just as the notes in music mean very little until they are set on the stave to give them pitch, so I have had to etch in a few details of the life behind these stories.

Today, many people live worlds away from the country and even life in the country now is very different from what it was in the early years of this century. To help to understand the book I have endeavoured to paint a picture of country life before the Second World War.

Today we hear a lot about abuse. We tend to think it belongs to the present day in our large cities and towns. However, here we have an abused little boy living on the moors when the century was young.

Writing this book has not been easy. There are two main reasons for this. Firstly, the stories were often told in a Yorkshire dialect and I had to have them translated! Incidentally, except for an odd Yorkshire word here and there I have tried to write in standard English. Secondly, the stories were not told in chronological order, and constantly during the writing of this book I was given material which had to be squeezed into what I had already written!

Although all the incidents in the book itself took place before 1937 and so very few characters will still be alive, nevertheless I have changed all their names to protect their identity. The only exceptions to this rule are William himself, and dear Jane and Joe whose praise cannot be sung too loudly!

A lot of my life has been devoted to children, either those I have taught or my own. I think the children of this world, generally speaking, have a raw deal! Therefore any profit I make on this book I have said I will give to the Save the Children Fund.

Finally, in spite of the difficulties, I have enjoyed writing this book. I do hope you will have great pleasure reading what I have written.

Chapter One

BLISSFUL YEARS

"D' yer want a babby*?" said Joe to his young wife, Jane, as he slopped water over his broad face.

"What do you mean Joe?" said Jane straightening up after setting the evening-meal on the table.

Joe dried his face.

"I met old Mrs. Smith int' village. Ses young Sybil's had a couple o' babbies. Doesn't know what she's going to do with 'em. She wondered if we'd like un since . . . .".

"Oh Joe! Do you mean we could have one here?" exclaimed Jane clasping her hands together in glee.

And that was how young William, the weaker twin, who was not expected to survive, came to live with the game-keeper and his wife. Jane and Joe had been married for a while, but no babies had come their way as yet. However, sure enough, as has happened many times before and since, shortly after William's arrival, Jane found she too had a baby on the way. In later years, Joe would tell William, with a twinkle in his eye, "We were given you as a sample!"

The date, dear reader or listener, is 1905. It was the beginning of a century that was to see so many advances in so many fields of knowledge. How hard it must be for people born at that time to accommodate in the mind such new inventions, as well as changes in everyday living! But in 1905 the Victorian period had barely finished.

The setting is the North Yorkshire Moors, one of, if not the largest area of heather moorland in England. Lastingham where William was born, and Gillamoor where Joe and Jane lived, are villages on the Southern edge of the moors, not far from the East to West, Scarborough to Thirsk trunk road. In Butler's "Lives of the Saints" we are told that, Ethelwald, King of Deira, gave St. Cedd a

"tract of land for a monastery in an inaccessible spot among the fells of Yorkshire. Here Cedd spent forty days in fasting and prayer to consecrate the place to God according to the custom of Lindisfarne, derived from St. Columba".

*Pronounce as in "tabby".

This was in 658 A.D. In 664 A.D. soon after Cedd's attendance at the Synod of Whitby

"he died at Lastingham during a great pestilence. At the news of his death thirty of his religious brethren among the East Saxons came to Lastingham to consecrate their lives where their holy father had ended his. But they too were carried off by the same pestilence, except one boy".

According to Derry Brabbs in "English Country Churches" St. Cedd's monastery was later sacked by invading Vikings. Later an Abbot called Stephen sought William the Conqueror's permission to rebuild the monastery. He finished the crypt which is a complete church in itself, St. Cedd being buried by the altar. However the monastery was never finished because Stephen took his monks to safer territory at York. The parish church on the site was eventually finished in 1228.

Joe was a giant of a man in every way. Even in his seventies he still had a tall, stout frame, a broad weather-beaten face and a generous heart. His heart was big enough to accept a weakling child into his home and care for it without recompense, long before the days of state benefits. This would be a magnanimous thing to do were a person wealthy, but how much more so Joe, a humble game-keeper for the local landowner.

For those of my readers who do not know very much about country-life, let me explain the role of a game-keeper. Keepers were employed by landowners to take care of their game e.g. deer and pheasants, so that when the shooting season came, the landowner and his friends would have plenty to shoot. This job would entail assisting pheasants in rearing their young as well as making sure that other animals and people (poachers) did not take them.

When one thinks of poachers, one immediately thinks of the male sex. However, Joe told William in later years, that one night he helped another game-keeper from a neighbouring estate in his work. The habitual poacher they caught was a seventy-one year old woman! Before one condemns her, let us remember that in those days she would not have a state-pension and she was probably catching the odd rabbit for her week's meat supply.

Jane was a slighter person than Joe, and she did not enjoy very good health. Before marrying Joe, she had been a maid in a major's household. Now she kept their little home clean and tidy, and was a "good contriver" at eeking out their meagre resources, William remembered in later years.

Joe called his Gillamoor home York Castle, showing not only his sense of humour and his belief in the statement "that the Englishman's home is his castle", but also his love of Jane in regarding her as his queen.

Anything less like a castle one cannot imagine. The house consisted of a single room downstairs with a stone-flagged floor and two bedrooms upstairs. This little home was rented. Apparently most lowly country folk did not buy their houses, but rented them from a plentiful supply. If homes stood empty for a while, there was no danger of them being vandalised or possessed by squatters.

A "clippy-rug" covered part of the floor. William remembers helping his "Aunt" Jane to make them. A clippy rug was a way of using up old outer garments like coats and dresses. These garments were cut into narrow strips and then pushed with a hand-tool into a sacking. Sometimes patterns were worked into the rugs, but other times the rugs were simply mottled. A quick shake out of a window or door freshened them up in the morning!

"And the oldt butler said ha ha ha ha ha!" laughed Joe when he reached home that evening. "He said 'have a drink, Joe' ha ha ha ha ha!" chuckled Joe again. "He said 'his lordship's never had such a good telling off in all his life' ha ha ha ha ha!" roared Joe again.

"Joe, for goodness sake, pull yourself together and tell me what all this is about!" said Jane exasperated.

So Joe explained that he had got permission to have an hour or two off work to join the now banned otter-hounds and their handlers! However, Joe had enjoyed himself so much that the day went and he scarcely knew it.

When Joe finally came face to face with his irate lord and master Joe spoke his mind and resigned. The butler, waiting on his lord and master at the time, was amazed to hear anyone address the powerful in such terms and when the door was safely shut offered Joe a drink for giving his master such a lecture!

"But Joe, do you mean you haven't a job and we've two bairns to feed?" cried Jane.

"Don't worry lass," reassured Joe, "I'll get out tomorrow and find something else!"

Joe was as good as his word and got a job as a gardener. He supplemented his income by clearing farmers lands of rabbits. Rabbits used to be a great nuisance early in the century, scores of them eating the precious crops before fertilisers and new research increased the yield of the fields. Then the disease myxamatosis was introduced from Australia later on in the twentieth century and the rabbit population was decimated. The present author can remember seeing scores of dead rabbits lying on the grass whilst on country walks. The first time Joe would attempt to catch rabbits in a particular field he would catch a lot, whereas the second time there would be fewer to catch and he would not make as much money.

"D'yer wonna come with me and set sniggles?" asked Joe of William when the lad was old enough to walk a mile or two.

"Oh yes please!" squeaked William as he grabbed his coat.

William had watched Joe garden before but he had never been out rabbiting with him. They walked through the village and pushed open a big, wooden farm-gate on the left.

"Is that a rabbit-hole?" asked William pointing to a hole under a hawthorn hedge which bounded the field in which they were walking.

"It is lad. I'll bring ferrets and nets another day for him, today we've got sniggles".

"Will the ferrets chase the rabbits out of their holes?" asked William.

"They will that, lad," answered Joe. "I'll spread my net out near the burrow and then I'll send down ferret and out'll dash the rabbit, straight into m'net".

It was a truly beautiful panorama which stretched out in front of them. The sun shining in a pastel blue sky heightened every colour. Above them were the moors, now purple clad being late summer. A white blob here and there marked where a moorland sheep was grazing. In those days there was not so much poisonous bracken about which is now causing concern in farming communities. Neither was the Forestry Commission formed and so had not planted the rows of coniferous trees which we see today. Further down the hills, in the valley bottoms, the heather gave way to lush green fields, a line of darker trees marking where water flowed through the dale. At their feet was a late hay crop with more wild flowers and herbs in it than we see today. Experts tell us weed-killers have seen to that. Bees went about their work here as they did on the moors returning to their hives put on the moors to make the lovely heather honey.

"What are we looking for?" asked William.

"We're looking for rabbit-tracks, lad, where they run across field," answered Joe.

After a few minutes Joe bent down.

"There, look lad, the rabbits have been dashing this way across field."

William looked. At first he saw nothing, and then he noticed that the grass was flattened a little in a certain place.

"And here's some of their droppings to prove it!" said Joe triumphantly.

He showed William the little dark balls on the grass. Joe dropped the bag he was carrying and proceeded to erect a sniggle.

Sniggles have now been banned in England, but they once used to catch rabbits running in their tracks. Basically a sniggle consists of a stick pushed into the ground to which is attached a loop of wire. The rabbit gets caught in it and has to remain there until the setter of them returns.

"Are we going home now?" asked William.

"Nay, lad, there is more than one rabbit to catch. I've a bagful of sniggles to set. We'll go home when they're set lad!" explained Joe.

They continued with their work and then started heading for home.

"When will you come back to see if we've caught any rabbits?" asked William.

"I'll have m'tea," said Joe, "and then late tonight I'll pop out and see if there's anything in sniggles".

"And what will you do if there is?" asked William.

"I'll pull their necks out!" said Joe.

That night the sun set for the last time for many small rabbits. It was also setting on this idyllic period in William's life.

Chapter Two

YORK

In about 1910, (William would be five), his mother, Sybil, married a York blacksmith. The twin she had kept, although stronger at birth, had not survived very long. One can only speculate why the boy died.

"I don't believe it!" cried Jane. "We've treated him as our own son these five years – kept him alive, not like his brother – got him out of nappies – got him to feed himself nicely – and she wants him back!"

"I know lass", said Joe, holding his distraught wife, "but he's her bairn and I expect we'll have to let him go!"

The day of William's departure drew nearer. The night before he was due to leave them Jane and Joe stood at his bedroom door to check he was all right before retiring, as, no doubt, all wise parents do. William was asleep, blissfully unaware of his future. Perhaps he was dreaming of the open moors, the village farms or evenings round the fire with sweet Joe and Jane in their cosy cottage. That night, (Jane told William years later), the couple cried themselves to sleep.

York is one of those places that is on every visitor to England's itinerary. It stands on a fertile plain with hilly areas the Yorkshire Dales away to the West and Yorkshire Moors away to the East. York is older than Lastingham, being inhabited in Roman times or perhaps even earlier. In the course of this century more attractions and facilities have been made in York, such as many museums and the university. When William, his mother and stepfather lived in York the tourist attractions were the River Ouse, ever likely to flood as its waters were swelled with rain falling in the dales, the old, very narrow streets often featured today on calendars, the stone city-walls one could walk on, the remnants of the castle and the magnificent minster. A "Fax-Pax" tells us that –

"York Minster is the largest mediaeval church in Northern Europe. Its central tower of sixty-four metres high is the largest lantern tower in Britain, and England's greatest concentration of stained glass from the thirteenth and fourteenth centuries can be seen in the minster, including the famous Five Sisters Window, while the magnificent East Window completed in 1408 by John Thornton of Coventry and displaying

over two thousand square feet of ancient stained glass is the largest in the world".

Of course, there was poverty in the great city as well just as there is in our cities today. The family rented two houses while they were in York, in Webster and Rhymer Streets. Passing an open doorway one day, William stared until he was threatened by the father, at the sight of a family drinking out of tins!

Drink too is not a new problem. William recalls a habitual drunkard who frequently called at their house, and who would ask him to sing for a penny, whereupon he would oblige with,

"Flannagan, Flannagan,

Take me to the Isle of Man again",

no doubt an old song no longer remembered and performed.

Perhaps this would be a suitable place to mention an old remedy for chests at this time. Lard and mustard were placed on material and stuck to one's chest, the plaster being held in place with strings! As one improved, small squares of this creation were removed piece by piece!

I have also been told of boiled onions being placed on one's chest in a similar manner! One must remember that these were days before the formation of the National Health Service, and old remedies would be tried before finally resorting to a doctor who would charge for his services.

William caught scarlet fever in 1913. It left him deaf in one ear, just as others have been similarly harmed with this disease. Fortunately this illness does not occur as frequently now.

It was while in hospital at York over Christmas that Santa Claus brought William a pop-gun. Another Christmas, at home, William found ashes from the fire in his stocking! To have forgotten the child at Christmas would have been bad enough, but to execute a plan to give him ashes is so mean and spiteful I find it hard to believe a mother could treat her son in this way.

An abscess under one ear caused William to be taken to hospital again. Without any anaesthetic his face was lanced and the pus extracted!

One can only wonder, in view of her future treatment of him, why Sybil wanted William back with her. She had managed five years without him, and William had been very happy with Jane and Joe, just as they had been sorry to lose him. Was it some vague sense of duty which told her she ought to care for and support her own child? Was it thoughts that in eight or nine years (children left school aged about thirteen or fourteen then) William would be bringing in a wage packet? Whatever the real reason was, judging by her treatment of him it would seem that her aim was to make the poor child thoroughly miserable.

William had been "dry" when he left Jane and Joe. Now he regressed and started bed-wetting and did so until he was fourteen! Jane thought it was lack of food which caused it, but perhaps it was unhappiness. Researchers have shown that children can regress if there is some crisis in their lives.

One happy memory of William's was being given by his school a tin of biscuits to mark the coronation of George the Fifth. George became King in 1910 and was crowned in 1911.

Neighbours in York suspected William was badly treated and alerted a children's organisation.

"William", called Sybil, "come here!"

William wondered what he had done wrong, and slowly made his way to his mother.

"William listen carefully. A lady is coming to see us this afternoon. When she's here I want you to do two things. Ask me for a penny and put your arm round me as if you loved me. Do you understand?"

"Yes", said William very perplexed.

"Just you dare forget!" shouted his mother.

That afternoon when the lady came and William was examined for bruises. Fortunately for Sybil, she found none. William forced himself to cuddle his mother and asked her for the coin. His request was granted. How different his mother seemed this afternoon, thought William. So, the charity organisation was hoodwinked into thinking that all was well between William and his mother and that the neighbours had over-reacted. No doubt Sybil thought she had been very cunning! Soon, with her husband out of the way and herself back on the moors she could get away with more ill-treatment of her first-born!

Chapter Three

WAR

With the outbreak of the First World War in 1914 the backcloth of William's life changed again. Many men responded to the posters declaring, "Your country needs you" and enlisted. The expression "take the King's shilling" was coined, because the ordinary soldiers were paid a shilling a day. For anyone born after 1971 when our coinage was changed, a shilling was equal to five new pence.

Blacksmiths were needed in the war-zone too and William's stepfather left his York home and job and made his way first to Aldershot, and then to Chatham, and finally to France. However his pay was far better than the soldiers just mentioned, because as well as an allowance for himself he was able to have four pounds a week sent home to his wife!

Now that her husband was in France, Sybil moved back to where her relatives were in Lastingham. William was nine. Two more sons had been born to her and her husband in York. She was able to rent a house in Lastingham for a shilling and sixpence a week (seven and half new pence!). She had been a cook and a maid, but now she turned her hand to washing to further increase her income. A local farmer employed her to do a day's washing for a week's rent. The farming household would run and fetch almost everything they could think of for her to wash! However Sybil soon learned how to make more money at washing! If she took in washing, each item could be charged for separately!

However, one of Sybil's faults was that she was easily led by others. Often a friend would arrive early in the morning and suggest that they forgot their work and took a horse and cart to Pickering seven miles away. Sometimes they went to Scarborough twenty-five miles away – quite a distance in those days! The friend was married to one of the men fighting in the war for a shilling a day, so no doubt Sybil with her superior income paid for her friend as well on these occasions!

It would be appropriate to note here that individual men with horses and carts did the work of moving people and goods about the country, before more modern forms of transport. Each man worked in a particular area, and so a parcel being sent a distance had to be transferred from cart to cart many times before it reached its destination. When the railways arrived they were still used to link small villages with main lines.

William attended the village school. The school had outside urinals as had many schools for a greater part of this century. An old pear tree overhung the metal roof of this building. In the Autumn the children in the school-room could hear when the wind blew pears off the old tree to deposit them on this roof! Hungry William readily admits to being one of the boys who asked on many occasions (in order to retrieve the pears), "Please may I leave the room?"

The school mistress came from Scarborough, but lived in the schoolhouse. She started to give William private piano lessons. However, just when he was beginning to make a little progress his mother stopped his lessons. She claimed she was short of money, but her husband and other family members felt she should have had a small fortune! Actually it had been rather a stupid idea of Sybil's in the first place to let William learn the piano because there was not an instrument in his home on which he could practise! In spite of being advised otherwise, his mother seemed to think a few lessons on the keyboard made one a pianist!

A little later on, William got a job as a paper-boy. It involved walking (only the wealthy had bicycles at this time) the one and three-quarter miles to Hutton-le-Hole to collect the evening papers and then bringing them back to sell in the village. William earned twelve shillings (sixty pence) a month for this, but he never saw a penny of it because his mother took it all! How times have changed! Can one imagine letting a very young teenager today walk three and half miles along dark country lanes? Can one imagine a young person being willing to do this, knowing that he would not be able to spend his earnings?

Sybil and her family attended church on a Sunday. How sad that she did not show love for her first-born through the week as she was taught to love others as oneself on Sundays! William seems to have been a useful boy in church, singing in the choir, and working the bellows to provide air for the organ. It is good to see that in spite of his harsh treatment he still had a sense of humour. Apparently, one Sunday he wondered what would happen if he stopped working the bellows. So he stopped working them, only to find that the lady organist popped her head round the corner and said to William,

"Give us some wind!"

For some reason William was sent to the Methodist Chapel on a Sunday as well as church! One can only wonder why! Was it to get him out of the way for an hour or two? The present author has known parents who behave in this way. Actually, William preferred the chapel. He thought one changed one's position too many times in church from standing to sitting to kneeling!

William loved the chapel anniversaries when the people celebrated their place of worship being opened a certain number of years. The organisers would go round the local farms for food contributions. No doubt other people would be conducting rehearsals. The village folk travelled round to all the anniversaries in the area: Lastingham, Gillamoor, Fadmoor and Hutton-le-Hole. In this area they were held from late May one a week into June. On the day there would be a concert-like service, followed by a delicious tea, including country ham sandwiches and fancy cakes. William remembers standing at the front on one occasion and saying,

"I'm only a little boy,
I've not stood up before,
But when I'm a bigger boy,
I'll tell you something more!"

However, behind this facade of normality, William was a badly treated, even abused boy. His mother employed many means at her disposal to make his life thoroughly wretched.

Every night it was William's job to go to the village tap (I believe it is still there now!) and draw two buckets of water. It was in a bowlful of this icy water that William and his two younger brothers had to wash, outside in the yard in every kind of weather! Their mother took her water indoors! One dreadfully cold winter, William got frostbite, and cream had to be applied.

At night the three boys slept on a mattress on the floor, their mother being unwilling to spend her wealth on a bed!

"She should have enough money to sink a battleship!" quipped William's grandfather.

He was often hungry only being allowed to walk round the table and smell the food rather than eat it! Other times his mother gave him marmalade to eat which she knew he disliked intensely! Some days when he went out to school hungry, a relative in the village would give him a little to eat, but there was trouble if his mother found out. One little incident, amusing if it were not so sad, was the time when William spotted a slab of creamy, yellow stuff on the table. The hungry child picked it up and bit into what he believed was cheese, only to discover it was household soap! No doubt he was in trouble for spoiling the soap!

"Usual amount of milk, Mrs. White?" asked the man delivering milk.

"Yes please, Mr. Peters!" replied Mrs. White holding out her jug.

William was tucking into a good breakfast in Mrs. White's house on his way to school! From where he was sitting, he could see Mr. Peters pour milk from a large, metal measuring container into his relative's jug.

Some days later William and his mother were at home when Mr. Peters came round with the milk.

"Hello there, William!" he began. "I saw you the other morning tucking into breakfast at Mrs. White's!"

William's heart sank. If only Mr. Peters knew his mother like he knew her, the milkman would not have betrayed him like this, he felt. Sybil glared at William but stayed her hand until Mr. Peters said,

"Goodbye!"

"What's this I hear?" she stormed, rushing at William, hand raised like a javelin above her head.

"It was just a cake. She just gave me a bit of cake!" blurted out William.

"Are you sure?" his mother hesitated.

"Yes!"

"That's all right then!" sighed his mother, the javelin slowly turning into a hand again.

If Sybil had done her duty and fed William, others would not have taken pity on him, and he would not have had to lie!

"Thank goodness that's done!" gasped William's aunt flopping in a chair.

"You must have had every pot and pan you own in that washing-up, Auntie!" exclaimed William.

"Well it mounts up you know," answered his aunt. "There was the family's pots, and the farm-men's, and then I've been baking as well".

"I'd better be going now, Auntie," said William.

"Wait a minute, William. Let me give you something. You certainly deserve it helping me with all that washing-up. Here, have this, and thank you again!"

His aunt pressed a shilling into his hand, and William, after calling farewell, started on his way home. William clutched his coin. What should he do with it? He knew perfectly well his mother would find it and keep it if he took it home. He did not want to spend it now on food, because he did not feel hungry, (his aunt had made sure of that!) If only there was somewhere he could keep his money other than at home, but still be able to get it when he needed it! Home came into sight. Oh where, oh where could he put his shilling? It would be so useful to have it on those bad days his mother gave him little or no food!

William delayed his walk home. He loitered around the outside of the joiner's shop. And then he saw it. In the joiner's shop's side wall, he saw a small hole. Yes, it went in! Yes, he could get it out again quite easily! Would anyone notice it there and take it, William pondered? He pushed it in again. No, he did not think it was very noticeable where it was in the hole.

Light-heartedly, William continued his journey home. Now he had a safe supply of cash for those bad days!

Over the next few years, William frequently helped his aunt to wash-up. After cooking a meal for many mouths, or after baking, offers of help with the washing-up are always welcome! The aunt invariably rewarded William with a shilling, with which he in turn replenished his "wall-safe". Then, on bad days, the hungry boy would go to his store and be able to purchase a little food with his coin, such as a packet of cream crackers!

Bathing was another opportunity for Sybil to treat her child roughly. Another relative called one day to help her to get the children ready for the Methodist Anniversary. However, Sybil forbade her to bathe William so he could have his normal rough treatment from his mother's hands! It is interesting to note here that the bath where the children were bathed was wooden and rectangular and was the same bath that was used to scald pigs (to remove their hair and skins when dead).

"Do you boys want to earn some money?" Mrs. Matthews asked William and some other boys in the village.

"What doing?" asked William.

"Picking gooseberries for three ha'pence a stone". (This would be an eighth of our five penny pieces for picking about seven kilos of fruit!).

"It's not worth pricking our fingers for!" retorted the quick-thinking William.

However, this was not the end of the incident. William's mother was informed, he was punished for his answer to Mrs. Matthews and had to pick the gooseberries whilst his mother pocketed the earnings! How heart-breaking for a child!

Summer holiday time came round. Sybil asked William, "Do you want to go to Scarborough or Gillamoor?"

William thought for a moment before replying. Knowing how his mother liked displeasing him, he gave his second preference not his first!

"Scarborough!" he replied.

"You can get yourself off to Gillamoor!" his mother snapped.

This was just what William wanted: to go to Gillamoor and visit Jane and Joe. He pretended to be downcast and moved slowly round the house and through the village. However, once out of sight of his mother, he ran like an athlete to that kind pair he loved! No doubt living with such an unloving mother made William very cunning!

It was William's job to light the open fire in a morning. Anyone who has had anything to do with coal or log fires will know that there are times when getting them to light is easy and other times when they will not make a merry blaze! William discovered that if he took a little candle-wax from the supply of unused candles it made the job easier! One day a relative called to borrow some candles and was supplied with them.

"Thank you Sybil", said the relative.

She started to talk to William's mother and as she did so her fingers fiddled with the candles. William in the room at the time, wished she would go, fearing that at any minute the missing inches of candles would be spotted!

"Hey, Sybil," said the relative, "look at these candles. They seem to be shorter than they should be!"

As you can imagine, this incident ended with William being punished.

One Sunday the boys were ready to go to church.

"Got you Tiddles!" exclaimed Dick picking up a small kitten.

"Oh Dick, it's doing diarrhoea down you!" cried Frank.

Dick dropped the animal.

"Oh Mam, look at the mess I'm in!" shouted Dick pulling a face.

Sybil came up and surveyed the scene.

"William, here's a job for you!" commanded Sybil very firmly. "Clean Dick up!"

So William found himself cleaning up the mess on his step-brother, as if he were a man-servant.

Other punishments Sybil meted out remind one of a concentration camp rather than a home! William had to stand still for long periods. If he relaxed and took his weight off one leg his mother would kick him! He had to wear clothes he disliked, his body became covered with scabs and he caught ringworm. (Ringworm was more prevalent at this time than it is now). "Health Education", a Ministry of Education pamphlet, says,

"In 1920, for example, the incidence (of ringworm) was fifteen times as great as in 1950".

She must have hated the poor child, because once she even spat in his mouth! Not content with abusing him herself, his mother taught her two younger sons to dislike William and encouraged them to tread on his toes!

On one occasion Sybil approached to kick William, but he saw her coming, and put his hand out to protect himself. Somehow his mother was taken by surprise, lost her balance, and fell into a bath of water on the floor! One has little sympathy for this harsh woman at this point! William fled from the house. He was filled with fear for the future after this episode! Late in the evening, an auntie finding him still up and out in the village, asked him why he was not heading for bed!

One can only hope that she accompanied him home and obtained a cast-iron guarantee from Sybil that the lad would not be punished for this wetting before she left!

Meanwhile the Great War continued. Sometimes William and other young men of the village were excused from afternoon school in order to help the farmers on their farms, because their farm-labourers were fighting in France.

Eggs were gathered from the village and sent to the fighting men across the Channel. Sometimes girls would write their names on the eggs before they were sent and occasionally a girl would receive a letter from a war-weary soldier!

News of the death of Edith Cavell reached the village school and touched all hearts. The children had a collection and bought a picture of her to hang in the school. "The Hutchinson Paperback Encyclopaedia" says of Edith Cavell, 1865-1915

"British matron of a Red Cross hospital in Brussels, Belgium, in World War 1, who helped allied soldiers escape to the Dutch frontier. She was court-martialled by the Germans and condemned to death. Her last words were, 'Patriotism is not enough. I must have no hatred or bitterness towards anyone'."

Chapter Four

AND SO TO WORK

In 1919 William was fourteen and left school. He spent the next year or two of his life as the village butcher's assistant in Lastingham. One must not imagine a modern butcher's shop, with counters, fridges, large windows and blinds. No, this shop was more like a shed!

One must also mention here how people did not waste things years ago. People took jars or tins to be refilled with treacle at the local shop, as well as empty sugar-packets to be refilled with sugar!

William worked every day, and was paid seven shillings and sixpence a week (about thirty-seven new pence). However, just as is mother took his earnings as a paper-boy, so now she took his wage!

One of William's duties was walking round the area delivering meat placed in a large, oval, wicker basket.

"Make sure this boy gets a drink of tea when he comes, because he delivers such tasty meat!" said Lady Young to one of her servants.

Giving William little rewards like tea was better for him than the extra coppers he used to earn for delivering meat, because even these were taken from him by his mother!

"You will stay an hour or two more, won't you, William?" said his boss as William was about to leave work.

"What do you want me for, Mr. Grisle?" asked the lad.

Mr. Grisle glanced round him to make sure no one had entered his premises. He put his hand on William's shoulder and lowered his voice.

"I've got an uncle of yours coming round just now. You know, the one that's a butcher and a jolly good slaughterer of animals too," began Mr. Grisle.

"You mean Uncle . . . . ?" piped William.

"Sh lad!" whispered his employer. "The war might be over, but there's still rationing in force. You are to keep quiet about all this, you understand?"

"Yes Mr. Grisle", said William in a softer tone.

The butcher walked to the door and looked out.

"He's just walking through he village now", he said to William, on entering his shed-like premises again.

Soon the three of them were inside and ready to begin. Mr. Grisle held the first beast to be killed, William a candle and the uncle, the tools necessary for the slaughter.

"I can hardly see", protested William. No doubt he was used to seeing in an evening with the aid of some kind of an oil lamp.

"Just so long as we can see what we're doing", retorted his boss. "Hold that candle more over here!"

It was hard to see that was happening in the candlelight, with people, animals and soon carcasses about, but that, of course, was the way Mr. Grisle wanted it. The beasts seemed to get stunned before they were killed.

"Now how much do I owe you?" said Mr. Grisle to the uncle when it was all over.

"It's five bob for each cow and one and sixpence for each sheep and pig", answered the slaughterer.

Five bob meant five shillings which is twenty-five pence in new money. One shilling and sixpence is seven and half new pence.

Mr. Grisle counted out the money to the uncle.

"Thanks again", he said. "I'll see you again in a few weeks!"

The uncle went on his way into the night, and Mr. Grisle was left to deal with the carcasses (cutting them into pieces) and William was left to deal with the entrails.

At this point we might pause and consider what these men were doing. When England is at war, many foodstuffs are rationed carefully. What a blessing they are, otherwise man, prone to being greedy, would buy as much as he could as the expense of his poorer neighbours! Farmers were allowed to kill a certain number of animals, so these men were obviously killing more than they had been allowed. Perhaps they had not been strictly truthful about how many had been bred in the first place! With extra meat they, no doubt, would either satisfy their own needs or use it to exchange for other needed goods on a black market.

Rationing does not cease the day peace is signed. It takes months or years before supplies are back to normal. The present author remembers sweets coming off ration about 1952 or 3 when she was in the junior school and being allowed to take and eat sweets in class to celebrate! This was seven years after the Second World War!

The men used candlelight to work. If what I am told is correct, they were lucky there was not some kind of explosion! My son tells how a fellow pupil's horse needed an operation. A biology teacher sought permission to take her class to watch the operation being performed. The veterinary surgeon before operating, checked that no one had matches and other inflammable goods on their person. He explained that when animals are opened, methane gas escapes which can be dangerous!

Just then William heard a small noise somewhere in the room. He looked up and discovered that Mr. Grisle was no longer in the shed. The noise continued. He was suddenly filled with fear: the fear caused by being alone in that dimly-lit shed with the sight and smells of guts all round him and fear of that persistent noise. A moment later he leapt back a pace as his eyes stared at a brown rat, perhaps eight inches long (twenty centimetres) with a tail nearly as long again, running across the shed floor, pick up a piece of intestine and return with it to where it came from!

William had heard many stories about rats and he feared and hated them. He had heard how they can jump at people's throats. Originating in Asia, they have managed to spread all over the world. On farms they will eat corn, steal eggs and kill chickens. They carry food-poisoning germs too.

William wondered what he should do. Would the rat, now well-fed, not return, or would he carry food away to its home, perhaps to young ones, only to return immediately for more! Then he had an idea. He sorted out a choice morsel, carried it like an offering to some god, to where he had first heard the noise, and placed it on the floor. He hoped, should the rat return while he was still busy in the shed, that the rat would take the offering and leave him in peace!

William returned to his work. Sure enough, a little later William heard the noise and looked up to see the rat making off with the morsel. So, William placed another offering in the corner. Indeed, William repeated his procedure several times in order to keep the rat away from himself and his work!

Meanwhile the men were returning from the war. Eye-witnesses said it was often a pitiful sight: lines of soldiers filing off trains, many of them wounded.

Sybil's husband came back to England too and once more took up residence and work in York. Sybil did not join her husband and live at York immediately, but she did two other things. She would occasionally go and spend time with him in York. The other thing was the baking! Now Sybil had many failings, but she was a good cook and baker. Indeed, that had been her job before she married. Sybil now used her skills to bake a wonderful array of goods for her husband, which she put in a large basket. It fell to William to arise early on a Friday morning and take this basket to a carrier who would take it to Kirkby-moorside. At Kirkby it would be put on a train for York, and so it would eventually reach William's stepfather!

The weeks rolled by, and the short, dull days of winter gave way to the long, glorious days of an old English Summer. William was making his way home after work and treading between the hens strutting freely in the open spaces of the village. As he drew near his house he heard shouts, and looking up saw several boys dashing out of the door and running round the garden. Then William remembered his mother had gone to her husband in York again. No wonder his brothers and their friends were able to run around without being constrained!

Suddenly an uncomfortable thought came into William's mind: the food! He knew his mother had left them some to eat while she was away. He quickened his steps and flung open the house door. The scene that met his eyes heightened his worst fears. A quick check round the pantry confirmed them! Yes, his brothers had evidently brought some school friends home with them, and with no mother around, had helped themselves to all she had left for her own children! There was nothing, absolutely nothing, left for him.

That was the proverbial last straw for William. After years of deprivation and abuse, now he found himself without food, and with his mother commandeering his wage, no money to buy any! He decided he was going to walk out on this wretched existence of his as Lastingham, and so, leaving the house, he walked, and walked and walked!

The lights had not been extinguished for the night in Lastingham before search parties were looking for William.

"You say you are asking at all the houses," said his Uncle Charlie to a searcher on being told of William's disappearance. "I'll gct my horse and cart out and scour the lanes for him. I'll go over to Gillamoor and see if he's at Joe and Jane's as well".

"Thanks Charlie!" said the searcher and returned to his task.

A little while later, Charlie was standing at Joe's door in Gillamoor.

"Nay, the lad isn't here!" said Joe. "I'll get dogs and I'll get out ont' moor and look for 'im!"

"That's good of you Joe!" said Charlie. "Let's hope someone finds him!"

Of course, the efforts of Joe and his dogs, Charlie with his horse and cart and the other searchers were all in vain. William was miles away.

"Did you find the lad then?" said Charlie's wife, Bessy, to him as he came through the door much later that evening.

"Nay lass! No one's seen him since he came home from work. Between you and me, Bessy," said Charlie starting to lower his voice, "I think the lad's committed suicide!"

"Oh no, Charlie, don't say that!" cried Bessy.

"Well look at the life he leads. His mother makes his life a misery. I tell you, it would not surprise me if by daylight they didn't find his body somewhere!"

"If they do", said Bessy, "it will be his mother's fault. She'll have that lad's death on her conscience all the rest of her life!"

Meanwhile, William had reached Pickering Station. The sun was descending rapidly in the Western sky and William knew that he ought to find a shelter for the night very soon. Seeing a bridge near the station he made his way to it. He was just about to rest his weary body when he jerked himself upright again! A dreadful thought had entered his head: there might be rats about! Imagine they ran over him while he slept! The idea filled him with horror!

He was still pondering what to do, when a shout startled him.

"Hey you! What do you want?"

William swung round and perceived a man dressed in station-master's uniform looking at him. William muttered something about meeting people getting off the Scarborough train.

"The Scarborough train!" gasped the station-master in amazement. "The last train from Scarborough came through an hour ago! You've missed them lad! Where do you come from?"

"I've walked from Lastingham", said William.

"You've walked from Lastingham! Why didn't you come by horse and cart?" asked the older man.

"I've no money", replied William.

"You must be tired and hungry", said the station-master. "Come along in and have a bite to eat!"

William could not believe his good luck! He followed the station-master meekly into the station-house. Inside, a woman was sitting at a table doing the tedious but rewarding job of topping and tailing gooseberries.

"I've a lad here", began the station-master, "has walked all the way from Lastingham to meet folks getting off the Scarborough train, and then he's missed them! Do you think you could make him a bit o' supper, Martha?"

Before long, William was eating a most welcome meal!

"I think you'd better stay here for the night," said the station-master. "You can't go back to Lastingham now".

"Oh thank you very much!" said William.

No doubt sleep would overtake William that night before he had time to reflect on the kindness of people like the station-master and his wife, Joe and Jane and Edith Cavell, compared with the self-seeking greed of others.

The next day, while William was eating a hearty breakfast, Martha sat down beside him.

"Now, I'm concerned about you walking all that way home", she said. "I want to know that you've got home safely. So, here is an envelope addressed to us, and I've even put a stamp on for you. Inside is a piece of paper and a bit of pencil. When you get back to Lastingham, just drop me a line to set my mind at rest. Promise you'll do that".

When confronted with such kindness, how could William not promise? So later on that day he arrived home in Lastingham. It was heart-warming to learn that some people had been concerned about his welfare!

However, things did not change much at home. A little while later Uncle Charlie met Mr. Grisle. In the course of their conversation Mr. Grisle said,

"I've just had to speak to that nephew of yours, Charlie!"

"Oh yes!" said Charlie. "What did you tell him?"

"I told him that I had a good business here and I needed someone to really put his back into his work. I didn't want anyone who sometimes seemed to lack "go"! In short, Charlie, I fired him!"

"I'm sorry to hear that!" said Charlie. "The poor lad doesn't get fed at home half the time, that's why he'll lack "go"!"

"Oh dear!" said Mr. Grisle feeling rather ashamed of himself, "I did not know that was the case!"

Chapter Five

NEVER WORK FOR RELATIONS

William spent the next year of his life working on his uncle's farm in the Lastingham area (not the uncle we have already met). It was 1921 and he was about sixteen.

In those days young men could leave home and go and work for a farmer. They could live in the farmhouse and have their washing done and their meals provided, as well as receiving a wage. Later on, if they married, there would probably be a cottage, owned by the farmer where they could live. They would also receive seventy stones of potatoes a year (that is between two and three pounds a day) and also two pints of milk a day, one from the morning milking and one from the evening.

However, if for any reason they stopped working for the farmer, they would have to get out of their home too. Hence these cottages were called "tied" cottages i.e. tied to the job. It is perhaps unnecessary to add that with mechanisation on farms these days fewer men and young lads work on them. In William's case, he worked for his Uncle Abner and Aunt Nancy for thirteen pounds a year, but what William particularly liked was the good food!

Breakfast would consist of bacon and eggs, bread and tea, no fruit or cereals (breakfast cereals at this time being largely unknown). Dinner at midday would be very much like a traditional school lunch, i.e. meat and gravy with potatoes and another vegetable, followed by a dessert. However, tea would consist of cold slices of bacon joint or cheese, with lots of bread and a great variety of home-made cakes. An apple or pear was eaten later in the evening.

In spite of the money that had been through Sybil's hands, it was his grandmother who provided his clothes for his new job and also whilst she was at the clothier's settled bills for his school clothes which she discovered had never been paid! However, as much as she wished otherwise, not being a wealthy woman, she had to charge William for these clothes past and present! How many children buy their own school clothes?

So, William started to learn farm-work. Over the years, he learnt to do about every job on the farm and do them well. A vet once remarked that William was so good with animals he should have been a vet. Squire Everly once stopped to ask who had thatched the haystacks they were so good, and yet a third person once commented that William grew cereals so well he wondered who the farmer was, William or his boss!

But this is leaping into the future. Now, he had to learn farming on his uncle's farm. There is a funny story from this period about William's ploughing! In those days one ploughed using two sturdy horses pulling a metal plough to turn over the soil. Anyone who knows anything about ploughing, will know that fields are ploughed in parallel lines. However, before William knew this he started at the edge of the field and went round the outsides of the field and slowly worked his way into the middle like a spiral!

About this time a decorator from Scarborough was decorating William's grandmother's house. Being a friendly man, he asked a lot of questions about her family. The interesting thing about the granny's answers was that she told him the names of all her children, but omitted Sybil, the child she had before she wed! When the James Bulger child murder was discussed on television in 1993, I remember a lady (I think from the University of East Anglia, but I am not certain) saying that people who perform cruel deeds have had something bad in their childhoods. One does wonder if Sybil was ignored, cruelly treated or humiliated in her childhood because she was born outside wedlock, and some-how this made her treat her first-born, William, in the way she did.

However, one need not imagine that a person with a bad child-hood will definitely perform cruel acts. In spite of all the physical abuse William suffered at hands of his mother, he was kind, generous and never violent towards his own children and grand-children! In fact he seemed determined not to let children suffer as he had suffered! Moreover, he liked to see animals well-treated too. He believed animals should have good food, be well-housed and treated with kindness. William said he could never be a butcher because he hated seeing the young lambs being killed.

About this time, Sybil moved away from her relations in Lastingham and joined her husband. They both moved to the Boroughbridge area about twenty miles North-West of York. (Boroughbridge was on the Great North Road until it was by-passed).

Meanwhile, William was not really happy on the farm. One reason was that all his relatives, those on Abner's farm and those on other farms, constantly expected William to help without pay. The second reason was the lies. Somehow, now Sybil had gone from the village, it seemed that her relatives wanted to erase both her and her son from their minds, and so all kinds of lies were told about William.

"Did you milk the cows this morning, William?" asked Nancy.

"Yes I milked them", replied William.

"Well you didn't do them, or not very well because I was able to get milk from them!" returned Nancy.

Now anyone who knows anything about mammals will know that milk is not suddenly produced before the young feeds, but is being produced all the time. So no wonder that when Nancy dashed out to the cows she was able to squeeze some milk from them! This, of course, was in the days when cows were milked by hand into a bucket, the milker sitting on a low stool.

"You haven't done much work this morning, William. You've spent all morning adjusting your boots!" complained Nancy on another occasion.

"If you had to wear boots like I've been given you would have been adjusting yours from time to time!" replied William.

But this truthful speech was to no avail. A letter was sent to his parents, accusing him falsely of, "cheek, drinking and being out of control", and asking them to take him from the farm! In reality, William was enjoying what little freedom he had in the Lastingham reading-room reading and playing Bagatelle!

Chapter Six

THE APRON STRINGS ARE CUT

William's parents responded to the request of their Lastingham relatives. They removed William from the farm and took him back with them to the Boroughbridge area. It was now 1922 and William was seventeen.

William soon found work on another farm, Mr. Thomas's. Generally speaking, farms at that time were either owned and worked by the farmer himself, or the farmer while living in the farmhouse and working on the farm paid rent to a greater or lesser land-owner. Mr. Thomas's nearly two hundred acre farm was rented.

When a farmer first took over a farm, he would ask his neighbouring farmers if they would give him a "ploughing day" to help him get started by turning over the land. It was like asking for a house-warming present! If the fellow-farmers obliged, (and I am told that people helped each other quite a lot) they would send a team of men and plough-horses to the newly taken-over farm on a particular day. The day would be in Spring, because farms changed hands on Lady Day, the 25th March. As for the horses, they would have their manes and tails plaited, and have coloured ribbons woven into the plaits.

Eighteen pounds a year was William's wage, five pounds a year more than he had received on Abner's farm. For some reason, alas, his washing was not done for him on the farm, (perhaps that was why his wage was more!). It was arranged that his mother would do his washing for him. A most unsatisfactory arrangement! So, after a day's work, William would find himself having to walk the six miles round trip to Sybil's to collect his clean washing. However, when he got there, he would find that his mother had been talking a lot of the day, and his clothes were not ready! She would promise to have them ready the next evening. The next evening would come and again it would not be ready! This would be repeated many times, causing William great inconvenience not having clean clothes, as well as having to spend his evenings walking six miles on top of a day's strenuous farm-work!

"She'll start washing on a Monday, and still be washing on a Saturday!" said Sybil's husband.

Before one glides over this criticism of Sybil, one ought to pause for a moment and consider what an arduous job washing was before the advent of the automatic washer.

Washing was usually done only once a week and done on a Monday. The day would start early because the water had to be heated first. This might involve having to light a coal or log fire in order to heat the water. When the water was very hot, it would be poured into a washing-tub, (if there was one), bath or barrel. Soap would be grated and added too! Then the white laundry would be added. These would be possed, that is worked up and down, with a poss-stick! A poss-stick was a copper hemisphere with holes in on the end of a wooden shaft. The holes helped the soapy water to circulate. Doing this is fun only for a few minutes! When one felt the washing should be clean, it had to be mangled to get rid of the soapy water and the soapy water saved for the coloured laundry!

Eventually, when all the different coloureds had been washed, the tub would be emptied and refilled with rinsing water! Everything would then be rinsed in a similar way. The final mangling had to be done many times to extract as much water as possible before drying the clothes outside.

What a business washing must have been! On top of all this, the dirtiest parts were sometimes soaped prior to washing. Some things had to be starched in yet another process! There were no tumble-dryers, of course, if it were a wet day. Finally, a lot of clothes, being natural fibres, needed ironing too! That was yet another more complicated operation than it is today.

William began to think about his future. His mother still claimed all his money, and so controlled the clothes he wore, where he went and his savings, or rather the lack of them!

With the farcical clothes-washing arrangements, his mother virtually controlled his free time too! William decided that his future was so bleak he had to change things. He would go and this time he would not return!

Farm-workers who lived in the farmhouse were not employed for life. A farmer would go to the hirings held in November and hire a farm-worker for a year. At the end of that year the time could be extended by mutual agreement.

When a deal had been struck between farmer and hired man at the hirings, the farmer would pay half-a-crown (twelve and a half pence) to the hired man as a sign of their agreement. This was called "God's Penny". After that the farm-worker would not receive any more money until he had completed his year's work, although he could ask for advances if in need.

Mr. Thomas wanted to employ an even younger youth and save money. That suited William who wanted to go, and so the two were happy!

One day, when William's time with Mr. Thomas was nearly over, he was working in a field of swedes. Suddenly, he heard a voice he knew only too well!

"So there you are William!" announced his mother.

"What are you doing here?" asked William stopping work and straightening up.

"I've come to remind old Thomas there that he's to give me your end of year wage, not you. I've also come to remind you, that when you're finished here, get yourself home and your father will get you something fixed up!"

William stared at his mother. She would be the last person in the world to whom he would reveal his plans.

"Yes, I'll stop you marrying 'til you're at least thirty, do you hear, boy?" sneered his mother, picking up one of the swedes by its green top and swinging it menacingly at William. "Do you hear? Do you hear?" she continued.

A mean, harsh, bad-tempered woman, swinging a swede in a field. That was one of the last pictures William has of his mother!

"But what am I going to do when your mother comes to collect your wage?" protested Mr. Thomas when William asked for his money a short while before he left.

William thought for a while, and then said, "Give her half".

How generous of him in view of all he had suffered! Mr. Thomas agreed with the arrangement.

The day of the departure arrived. William was up and packed extremely early. He wanted to be off the scene before his mother arrived for his wage and could alter his plans! William's train left the station at seven o'clock. His mother's came into it at nine o'clock! William's secret destination was Northallerton, about twenty miles North of Boroughbridge, where he had obtained yet another job on a farm.

That night it snowed. William spent it huddled on Bradbury Station in County Durham (another thirty miles North!). How he came to be there I can only speculate! At this distance of time I think William is a little hazy on this point! However, he reached Northallerton and more importantly, had finally cut those apron strings!

Chapter Seven

FIRST LOVE

Northallerton, like Boroughbridge and York, is situated on that fertile, flat land called the Vale of York *(see Chapter Two)*. It is a busy market town with a large church. When Yorkshire was divided into North, East and West Ridings, Northallerton was the county town for the North Riding.

The three hundred acre farm which Mr. Oldcorn farmed was his own. It was a mixed farm, that is he reared livestock as well as growing crops. Having many different animals, growing a variety of crops, meant there was always plenty of work on the farm in the days of horse, not tractor power. The farm kept at least nine horses to allow for changing horses (to get a fresh set) two or three times a day. As for people in the farmhouse, they started rising as early as five o'clock in the morning.

Mr. Oldcorn was a pleasant gentleman, but his wife was one of those people (and sadly they can be found today) who are concerned with social class! They had three children, two boys and a girl. One son was married and gone from the farm, but Norman and Pearl, twenty-six, were both still at home. They did not have outside work, but helped on the farm. As well as William, they employed another farm-worker, Bruce.

William started to work for Mr. Oldcorn in 1923 when he was eighteen. He worked for fifteen shillings a week (seventy-five new pence). This was the first money in his life he had been able to earn and keep!

After a little while he was able to buy the clothes he wanted. For farming, he wore a tweed jacket and tweed breeches. The breeches were fastened with seven buttons under the knee. On his lower legs he wore leggings made of leather or boxcloth, (a very closely woven material). These overlapped the breeches and were fastened with five buttons. The leggings, being tightly bound like this, prevented insects, adders or thorns getting up trouser slops. Under the jacket he wore a blue, cotton smock. How conservation-minded and economical some people were in those days! William tells how he used to have fresh toes knitted onto his woollen socks!

How times have changed too as far as paying for goods is concerned! William tells how one would order clothes from a tailor and not pay for them until the end of the farming year, when one was paid one's wages! Then, the tailor would invite you in for dinner when you had settled your accounts!

When meal-times came, the family and farm-workers ate in the same room, although the latter had separate tables. The farm-men were given pint-pots to drink from whereas the family had tea-cups.

At Christmas time, Mrs. Oldcorn used to invite all the local farmers sons to a big party in the farmhouse. On the surface it was joining in the Christmas spirit, whereas in reality it was trying to introduce Pearl to a suitable mate! William and Bruce were excluded from these occasions, and had to eat brown bread and butter in another room!

Still on the subject of food, William has also experienced farm-men being given different bread from their employers. The employees bread was a very course bread, no doubt from a cheaper, inferior flour.

In the evenings, Bruce was responsible for the cows, and William the horses.

"I'll give you a hand with the horses, if you give me a hand with the cows", said Bruce one night.

"All right", agreed William.

On the surface this seems like a piece of co-operation between the farm-workers. In reality Bruce had another motive in asking for William's help.

In those days, roadsters (tramps) walked the country lanes and when evening came found shelter in the out-buildings of farms, sleeping in the hay. Of course, they were putting themselves in a very vulnerable position when the did this, because the farm-staff, wanting hay for their animals, would obtain it on the end of a spiky hay-fork! To save themselves from being impaled in this way, they would sit up and shout out, when someone entered the dimly lit building. For the farm-worker, it was an eerie feeling entering a pre-electric barn and not knowing whether or not you were alone in it. Thus, Bruce wanted company when he did his evening work.

The cows being done, they made their way to the horses. As if to prove he was a big, strong man and not afraid of anything, (like tramps), Bruce started boxing the horses!

"What are you doing that for?" asked William.

"I feel like a fight", answered Bruce.

"Give over man, that's not how you treat horses!" exclaimed William.

This behaviour on the part of Bruce was repeated night after night. One night, William was putting hay in the rack of a hefty plough-horse and Bruce was boxing the other end of the horse! Suddenly, the horse reacted to the boxing and reared. Standing on its hind legs its front legs swayed about in the air over William.

"I've told you man, give over!" yelled William, wondering how he could escape from those hefty hoofs in a narrow stable. (One blow from the horse on his skull could kill or seriously injure him!). Mercifully, William managed to cower in a corner and eventually the horse brought its hoofs down again.

"That's the last time you help me with the horses!" exclaimed William firmly. "I could have been killed then!"

The next night the household were in bed, (the farm-workers shared a double-bed for warmth in winter and had single beds in summer!).

"Bruce, you've never fed those cows!" shouted Mrs. Oldcorn.

"I have!" replied the liar.

"You haven't", argued Mrs. Oldcorn. "Listen to them!"

Sure enough, one could hear the cows in the byre clamouring for their supper! Bruce had been too afraid of the unknown to enter the cow-house on his own!

William had settled quite well at Mr. Oldcorn's. He had now been there about half a year and it was Springtime. William was making his way back to the farmhouse. The air was full of bird-song. (Have you ever noticed how, only a few weeks after Christmas, when the days have only just started to lengthen a little, the birds start to sing very early in a morning?). The leaf buds on the trees which had been dormant all winter were opening to clothe the hedgerows and copses with that lovely lime-green they wear for only a few weeks. Early Spring flowers like primroses, cow-slips and celandines were under the hedges and by the roadsides. (Again, have you ever noticed how many early Spring flowers seem to be yellow?).

William gazed at the fields as he walked along. It was good to see the seeds he had sown growing. In the case of the corn crops, he had actually sown them like the sower would have in Bible days, that is, carrying a bag of seed round his neck, and plunging first his left hand and then his right hand into the bag, and grabbing a handful of seed flinging it onto the land. He had used a drill (a seed-sowing machine) to sow the hay-seed and the swedes. However, the potatoes had all been planted by hand individually. Soon the potatoes and swedes would need weeding.

In another field the year's new lambs were skipping. How white they were compared with their dirty, long-fleeced mothers who had borne all the weather and mud of the winter! Norman looked after the sheep. On reaching the farm orchard and yard Pearl's young chickens were running about with the older hens. Everywhere there was new life!

Perhaps at this point we ought to pause and describe our hero now that he has grown to manhood. William was a short, broad man but very strong. He had mid-brown hair and a broad, sunburnt, amiable face, the most striking feature of which was his clear, blue eyes.

As William strode through the farmyard he noticed one, no two, no three, no several of Pearl's young chickens opening their mouths in a peculiar way.

"Ah, there you are William!" exclaimed Pearl. "I want you to help me with my chickens. They've got gape".

"Yes, I've just noticed they have", answered William.

Gape is a disease of young chickens which causes them to open their mouths, hence the name gape.

"We've got some stuff in the house, so could we do them straight away?" asked Pearl.

"Well, if it's all right with Mr. Oldcorn", began William.

"You go ahead, lad, help Pearl with the chickens", said Mr. Oldcorn, also in the farm kitchen at that moment.

Pearl put a little bottle of liquid and a small brush in her pocket, and then she and William went out to try and catch the infected birds. After chasing all over the yard and orchard, at last they satisfied themselves that all the poultry they wanted were shut up in a henhouse to be treated! They went into the hen-house, and then while William gently lifted up a young bird and opened its beak, Pearl carefully painted the liquid on the creature's throat.

"Now let me do the painting!" said William, when Pearl had done several.

So they exchanged roles and William painted the little birds while Pearl held them.

At last, all the infected chickens had been treated, and had been let outside again.

"Thank you so much, William", said Pearl sweetly.

"I'm glad I could help", replied William.

Suddenly Pearl gently put her hand on William's shoulder.

"You know you are sweet and kind", she said. "I'm very fond of you".

William looked at her and then said truthfully, "I'm very fond of you too, Pearl".

And then, in the privacy of the henhouse, William gently took Pearl in his arms and kissed her.

"We'd better be getting back to the house", said Pearl several kisses later. "What with catching the chickens, and then painting them, we've been here ages, and they'll be looking for us just now!"

So the two very happy young people made their way back to the farm-house. William could not recall when he had been so happy. Perhaps he had not been so happy since those far off days with dear Jane and Joe on the moors.

One day William was sitting in a barn when he happened to see a fox go past the half-open door. He quickly got to his feet and made his way to the door and out to the farmyard and orchard. What a dreadful sight met his eyes! The fox had snapped the heads off four chickens in that space of time! Apparently foxes do this sometimes, and come back later to collect the bodies! However, if the farmer saved the bodies and showed them to the local hunt, he would be paid compensation for them! That is like the hunt paying the farmer because they failed to catch the fox that attacked his poultry. Perhaps it is also to prevent the farmer taking the law into his own hands, and going out to shoot foxes. The hunt would rather catch them themselves and so have some fun!

William also heard how on a neighbouring farm, the farmer accidentally shut his hens out one night, and twenty hens were killed by foxes by the next morning!

The weeks rolled by and it was now Summer. The leaves on the trees and bushes had changed for another year from lime to dark green. In the hedgerows the Spring flowers were gone and had been replaced by the stately foxglove, the delicate wild rose and the beautiful pink campion to mention only a few. The cuckoo, now returned from Africa, could be heard somewhere in the distance.

How strange the adult sheep looked since their long fleeces had been shorn from them! The new lambs now had more wool than their mothers!

While the other crops continued to grow, the hay-harvest had begun. First a reaper, (machine), had cut the hay and then after it had had chance to dry, it had been turned to dry it still more. Next it had been raked together with a horse-rake. Bruce and Pearl were now riding on a cart down to the hayfield, to fork the dried grass up onto the cart. They would then take it away to form a hay-cock before a hay-stack was made.

These days, however, we do not see many haystacks at the edges of fields. The reason is that hay needs sunshine to dry it, and this can be difficult to get in some English Summers! So farmers are treating the cut grass differently. They are compressing it and sealing it in black plastic bags for example, while it is still green. This pickles the grass and keeps it until it is required.

When they reached their work-place, Bruce jumped off the cart so that he could do the heavier job of lifting the hay onto the cart, whereas Pearl on the cart could do the easier task of putting it in position on the cart.

"That's a nice pair of ankles you have there! You know one gets a bit of a worm's eye view down here!" exclaimed Bruce as he raised some hay on his fork towards Pearl.

Pearl did not answer, but felt herself blushing.

"By, I've got you blushing now, haven't I?" went on Bruce enjoying himself.

They worked for a little while and then Bruce began again.

"By, that's a shapely pair of calves you have Miss Pearl. It'll be all the exercise you get on this farm. It makes calves muscley, you know!"

"Just get on with your work Bruce!" said the poor girl colouring again.

"Oh am I embarrassing you?" tormented Bruce.

Just then a gust of wind blew, disturbing Pearl's dress.

"By, that's some mighty fine lace you have there!" continued Bruce. "Just right for a farmer's daughter!"

"Bruce!" screamed Pearl.

"I'm getting you mad now, aren't I!" teased Bruce. "Can I have a better look at that lace?" persisted Bruce, stretching out his hand towards Pearl's underwear.

"Bruce please!" screamed Pearl again, now almost hysterical as she backed away.

"All right, all right", he said. "I'll get on with my work!"

Later that day, Pearl and William were together.

"I have told my parents I am not working in the hayfield with Bruce again!" declared Pearl. "And I'm not standing on the hay-cart again!" she went on.

"By all means don't work with Bruce in the hayfield, but you can trust and work with me", reassured William. "You must stand on the cart though, because lifting the hay from the ground is too heavy a job for any woman. You'll be all right up there with me!" reassured William.

"Now Mrs. Oldcorn and I are going away for the weekend", said Mr. Oldcorn one breakfast-time to the assembled company of Pearl, Norman, Bruce and William, "and once more I'm leaving everything in your very capable hands".

"Well, that's sixteen cows milked between us Pearl!" exclaimed William one morning that weekend.

"Let's go up to the farmhouse for a snack", suggested Pearl.

It was a lovely morning in early Autumn. The sun was shining and so all the trees looked their best in their innumerable Autumn shades of yellow, orange and brown. Groups of swallows seemed to be gathering, no doubt to make their long journey to Africa. As for flowers, they were nearly finished for the year, but here and there one could find an odd late specimen. The hedges, however, as if to compensate for the lack of flowers, were full of wild berries: the blood-red haws, the scarlet-red hips and the black brambles to name only a few. (Haws and hips are the fruits of hawthorn and wild rose respectively).

In the fields the potatoes would soon be spun out of the ground with a spinner to be gathered up by the potato-pickers, whereas the swedes, would all have to be lifted separately by hand.

However, it was the corn-harvest that was engaging the minds of farmers at that moment. Some corn had already been cut with a binder, had been tied into sheaves and was standing with other sheaves in the fields drying and waiting to be taken to a corn-stack. This lovely rural view is only a scene now in old photographs and paintings, since these days the combined-harvester cuts the corn and separates the grain moments later. It is worth noting here that the corn-harvest seems to be a little earlier in the year than it used to be, because farmers are growing earlier maturing varieties. Yes, it would soon be threshing day. What a day that would be! Full of machines, steam, men, dust, work and sweat! Threshing day would be in November. A steam-engine would arrive at the farm (these machines went from farm to farm) and had to be fed with coal to heat the water, to make the steam, to work the threshing-machine, to get the grain from the corn! There would be another threshing-day in March. The grain obtained then was better than the November's for sowing in the fields.

As for food on threshing-days, William reports joints of beef weighing twenty-eight pounds being bought to feed sixteen men sitting in two rooms.

"I'm so glad you suggested that I started saving with a building-society, Pearl", said William.

"Yes, it's good to have a little money out of the house where it can't be spent or stolen", replied Pearl.

"It's good to even have money!" said William.

"Yes, it must have been awful for you, doing all the work you did, and then your mother taking your money!"

"Let's forget my mother! She doesn't know where I am, and I'm happy here, earning money and being with you, Pearl!"

"That's sweet of you, William!" whispered Pearl. "If you can forget you have money in the building-society, you'll be surprised how it grows! And of course when you want to buy a house, they give their savers preference, you know!" continued Pearl.

"Well, as I said", replied William, "I'll always remember that you were the one who started me saving!"

————————————

It was Winter, the end of nature's, and the end of the farming-year. If one gazed from the farmhouse bedroom windows one could see the dark trunks and branches of the trees set against the pale grey sky. At a lower level were the hedges now trimmed for winter and beneath the hedges the dead brown vegetation of the year's flowers and grasses. In a field a man was ploughing using two sturdy horses to pull the plough. Scores of birds followed him, ready to seize grubs in the soil the moment they were revealed. Nearer the farmhouse, another man was shutting in the poultry for the night, out of the way of foxes. A lot of poultry had been killed for the Christmas that had just gone so there were fewer around.

"This evening, let's play that game you taught us William", said Pearl.

"Do you mean Whist?" asked William.

"Yes", replied Pearl.

The suggestion was met with general approval in the farm-house. So, when all had completed their outside chores, they settled themselves in the sitting-room. In front of them was a real log fire roaring up the chimney as the wind outside drew it up. It is a lovely feeling sitting beside such a fire, while the wind chases about outside, and knowing that one has not got to go out again that night, as well as knowing one's crops are safely gathered in.

"Now, Whist is best with four people", began William.

"All right, Bill, I'll not play this game", said Norman obligingly.

"I won't either", said Bruce.

"Are we going to play with partners, like you showed us?" asked Pearl.

"Well, Whist is usually played that way", answered William.

"I'll be your partner then", said Pearl eagerly.

"I expect that means we are partners, my dear", said Mr. Oldcorn to his wife.

William dealt the cards and they picked them up.

"Well, I might as well_____on these!" exclaimed Mrs. Oldcorn disgusted at her cards.

"Really, my dear, what a dreadful thing to say!" exclaimed a shocked Mr. Oldcorn.

Mrs. Oldcorn was, I am sorry to say, a bad sport; one of those people who forget that a game is simply that!

The game commenced. William and Pearl scooped trick after trick towards themselves. It was a mixture of good hands of cards as well as skilful playing. Needless to say, they were the winners.

"We make a good team you and I!" exclaimed William when it was over.

All of a sudden, Mrs. Oldcorn turned to the young couple and stared at them. It were as if she had been blind until that minute; blind to the lovely relationship that was developing between her only daughter and William, the farm-worker.

It was about this time that disaster struck the farm. What was it? It was the dreaded foot and mouth disease. How did they know their animals had the disease? They knew because cloven-footed animals dribbled at the mouth and had sores between their divided hoofs. (A horse has a circular hoof, whereas an animal such as a pig has its hoof divided into two parts). How did the outbreak of the disease come about? Rumours abounded in the area. There was a report that a man had been seen running away after leaving some infected animal bones on the farm. There was another report that Pearl had been visiting another infected farm and had sat on the knee of a farmer's son! Could it not be cured? One Irishman claimed that animals which were treated with tar on their hoofs and salt in their mouths, were stronger beasts afterwards. However, government rules do not allow animals to be treated (now or then). Instead, a hole was dug in a field, and infected animals were killed, thrown in the pit and then burnt. The fire smouldered for weeks! Other cloven-footed animals on the farm which were not infected were killed for meat.

Various other measures were taken to prevent the disease reoccurring or spreading. Overalls and germicides were provided for men to spray the insides of farm buildings. This being done, they were not allowed to keep animals again for several months! If they wanted to leave the farm for any reason, their cart-wheels had to be brushed with a germicide. As for their milk supply, now not having their own, they had to get it from a neighbouring farm, the milk being left in the lane for them to collect.

One day, Mrs. Oldcorn said very seriously, "You know, William, we are farmers and Pearl has to marry a farmer's son".

"You mean . . . . ", began William.

"Yes", interrupted Mrs. Oldcorn, "that's exactly what I mean!"

The next time the November hirings came round, Mr. Oldcorn decided that he would not employ William another year (he had been there three years) but he would employ a younger and less costly youth.

So, William left Mr. Oldcorn's farm and his first love, Pearl. It was 1926 and he was twenty-one.

Perhaps my modern readers will ask why Pearl and William did not marry and disregard her mother's wishes. To this I answer that although there were exceptions, nevertheless many young people years ago went along with their parents wishes in matters of marriage and careers. I also understand from William that had Pearl displeased Mrs. Oldcorn and married William, she would have lost her third of the farm on the death of her parents.

Chapter Eight

GIRLS GALORE

After leaving Mr. Oldcorn's farm, William stayed in the Northallerton area and got a job on Mr. Ingledew's farm. It was 1926, he was twenty-one, and he was paid a pound a week.

Nine people lived on the farm including William, although at busy times in the year Mr. Ingledew employed extra men. Mr. Ingledew had had some mental trouble and had been in some institution because of it. However, he was now out and running his farm, although some would say he still had some peculiar ways. (I add at this point, do not we all have some ways which seem odd to others?). Mrs. Ingledew told William she hoped he would help her husband on the farm and make allowances for him in view of his medical history.

Mr. and Mrs. Ingledew had four children, three girls and a boy. The other two members of the household were Mr. Ingeldew's father, now blind, and Miss Andover. Miss Andover was a farmer's daughter. Falling from her pram as a baby had left her with some peculiar ways too!

"Do you see the way she eats?" Mrs. Ingledew asked William, and so pointed out to him her rather strange mouth movements.

However, Miss Andover was able to earn her living and did a lot of heavy work in the farmhouse.

Mrs. Ingledew started bringing out to William cups of tea as he worked about the farm.

"My, she likes you!" chorused the casual workers when the lady was out of earshot and William was drinking his tea.

Whether or not William had regarded these cups of tea as anything other than drinks, before this chorus, I do not know.

Later on, the lady's intentions were clarified. They were working together in an out-building plucking the feathers from the Christmas poultry. There were feathers everywhere: in the sack they were putting them in, on the floor and floating in the air! Some would have said that in a haze of feathers one could be excused for catching the other's hand when putting feathers in the sack, but William knew that those touches were most certainly not accidental touches!

On another occasion, Mrs. Ingledew asked William to help her pull off her tight boots. When William obliged, she revealed a shapely leg to him! I am happy to write that William did not succumb to the advances of this lady. One does have a certain amount of sympathy for her, living on an isolated farm, and no doubt frustrated at times by the people around her as described earlier, but nevertheless it was wrong to try to lead a young lad astray. One wonders, actually, from where William got his moral code, in view of his childhood.

A certain young lady named Kate, working in a Northallerton sweet shop, did, however, interest William. Alas! After one date the young lady explained that although she wanted to remain friendly with William, she did not want to take the relationship any further. Instead, she was interested in a tall policeman! William has always joked that he had 'duck disease' i.e. his bottom was too near the ground like a duck's, preventing him from being tall!

At last William met Beatrix, a young lady who was as interested in William as he was in her, and whose heart was her own to give to whom she chose. They were soon good friends and seeing each other frequently.

Where did couples go when they met in the nineteen twenties and thirties? The answer I am given is to dances, on walks and to the picture-house. The latter, of course, were more plentiful in the days when people did not have television in their homes. Going out to see moving pictures was then a novelty. As for dances, William calls them the "Sixpenny Hops!"

"There was dancing and dancing", he explains. "Real dancing and just dodging about the floor!"

Of all the farmers for whom William worked, Mr. Ingledew seemed to need the vet for his animals most often. William does not know why this was so. Perhaps he did not trust his own judgement and so liked another opinion.

On one occasion Mr. Ingledew was worried about a calving cow.

"Get on the bike and tell the vet to come," said the farmer to William.

Soon the three men were tending the distressed cow. As it turned out, it was a sad and messy business. The calf had to be cut away a piece at a time! Antiseptic was used by the bucketful!

"What are you doing with those buckets?" Mr. Ingledew asked William when it was all over.

"I'm cleaning them, and putting them upside down on the fence for the frost to take the smell away", replied William.

"Bah!" exclaimed Mr. Ingledew, "you won't do so badly if you never taste anything worse than antiseptic!"

"I hope to taste much better things than antiseptic!" retorted William.

The next morning, when the buckets William had had to leave had been used to milk the cows and convey the milk to the breakfast table, one of the little girls said,

"Oh Mammy, this milk's not nice!"

Mrs. Ingledew looked reproachfully at William.

"I hope you had the sense to clean those buckets out properly last night!" she said to William.

"I did", said William, "but your husband didn't!"

"William, I want to see you later", said Miss Andover.

"All right, Miss Andover", replied William.

When the two were alone together, Miss Andover said,

"William, if ever you want a farm of your own I could let you have the money to make it possible".

"Oh Miss Andover", replied William, "that's very kind of you, but I really want to stand on my own feet".

"All right, William, but the offer's there!" returned the lady.

How generous of the lady! How she liked William and wanted to help him!

William continued to court Beatrix. He frequently visited her home, sometimes treating the whole family to fish and chips. Every week he would bring lovely, fresh farm butter from the farm where he worked to Beatrix's mother and she would pay him for it.

Many farms made their own butter at that time. The milk from the cows was put through a separator to extract the cream. This cream was then stored in a cool dairy until there was enough to have a butter-making session. The cream was poured into a wooden churn, supported in a stand, and then the churn was tumbled by turning a handle until one could feel a lump of butter was present rather than liquid cream. This could take several hours or only a few minutes.

There was another churn like a barrel. However, instead of being turned end over end as described, the barrel simply rolled. I am told that the former kind made butter-making quicker and easier.

Salt was added and later, the butter-milk was drained off through a hole. Finally, the hunk of butter was removed from the churn, and put on a table. Here, using patterned, wooden butter-pats, separate pounds of butter were removed from the slab, shaped, had a pattern put on their tops, and placed on greaseproof paper ready to be taken to the market or shops to sell.

Writing of loads to be taken to sell, what great weights men carried in the past! William used to carry seventeen stone of maize up flights of steps at Mr. Ingledew's. (If a small lady weighs about eight stone, seventeen stone is like carrying two such ladies!)

My own husband working in a bakery reports how weights to be carried have decreased over the years, about five stone being the maximum weight now. More recently the European Union has introduced laws to govern how much people can be expected to carry.

Once more, Miss Andover offered William money to run a farm of his own, and once more he replied as before.

William decided he would like to marry Beatrix and the two became engaged.

"So, you're getting engaged!" said Miss Andover. "Well, I've placed your suit as usual under your mattress!"

"Thank you, Miss Andover", replied William.

Poor Miss Andover! She had the erroneous idea that suits placed under the mattress of sleeping people pressed the clothes properly! William knew from bitter experience that this was not the case! However, he knew she meant well, and so said thank you, not having the heart to tell her otherwise!

About this time Beatrix's mother turned to William to borrow money to pay the rates, in spite of the fact that she had sons of her own!

One day, William was cutting the hay in a field with a reaper pulled by a horse, when shots rang out in the next field. No one was shooting William, but rather men were shooting rabbits. However, it was enough to startle the horse. The horse started to bolt, as if its tail were on fire, William sitting on the reaper-seat being taken along too! William was a wonderful horseman; he can never remember being taught to ride, just like one cannot remember learning to walk. He had the presence of mind to direct the horse in great zig-zags across the field, until it had calmed down and would work normally again.

Yet a third time did Miss Andover offer William money in order to manage a farm of his own and as before he declined the offer. I find this a little surprising, particularly so now that William and Beatrix were engaged to be married. Again, when one thinks of how William was deprived of money as a boy and youth, it is amazing he did not accept the lady's offer. One must also add, how noble of him not to have taken advantage of this lady who was perhaps not as intelligent as she might have been as a result of her accident.

It was now that Beatrix's mother started to cause trouble. It began when she could not pay for the week's butter, so payment was left until the following week. The second week she still could not pay, and so it was left until a third week. When the third week came, there was a dispute about how many weeks were owing. Apparently these arguments became frequent. In the end, in order to save William from this hassle, Mrs. Ingledew prevented him selling the butter to the mother! As for the money for the rates, which William loaned her, it remains unpaid to this day!

After two years, Mr. Ingledew wanted a different farm-man (perhaps he had an inkling how fond his wife was of William!) and William was temporarily out of work.

The welfare state, with unemployment amongst other benefits, was not created until 1947. Before that time what unemployment benefit there was, was not uniform across the country. However, William was lucky enough to get it.

"Why haven't you bought me a birthday present?" asked Beatrix when William met her on her birthday.

"Beatrix, you forget, I haven't a job now", replied William.

"But you have money in the bank!" she scolded.

All of sudden, William did not see Beatrix before his eyes, but the spectre of his greedy mother rose up instead! He had not escaped from Sybil in Boroughbridge only to find himself in the clutches of another grabbing woman in Northallerton! So William broke his engagement with Beatrix, and went elsewhere to look for work.

The world seems strange and empty when one parts from a beloved friend one has known for months or years. However, the more William pondered on it, the more he felt he had done the right thing.

He recalled how her brother, who was a commercial traveller, would go to London and return with cases of lovely fashions, including furs! (I do not think people in the nineteen-twenties thought about animals having to die for us to acquire their skins!) Beatrix would put her arms round William an ask,

"What are you going to buy me William, darling?"

The young man would let her have some of the beautiful things from her brother's case. It sickened him now to think of the money he had spent on her.

"I would never have had any money with her for a wife and her family for in-laws!" thought William.

William was also glad that he had been able to wean himself away from Dirk. He had met Dirk in Northallerton and the two had become great drinking partners. However, after a few weeks William had been shocked to discover how little money he had left of his wage when he went drinking repeatedly.

"I gradually phased him out!" William recalls.

What determination!

Chapter Nine

THE END OF AN ERA

In meditating upon the last chapter, one feels that had one magnified and developed certain incidents one could have made a better story! However, one has to remember that one is not writing a novel, but a life story, and then only the early part of it.

If one looks at a map of North-East England, one will see that between the River Tees flowing Eastwards into the North Sea, and the Northern edge of the North Yorkshire Moors, there is a belt of lowland. It was in this good agricultural country that William got work and spent his next few years.

William was twenty-three in 1928, the year he went to work for Mr. Skinner. His wage was still a pound a week as it had been when he had worked for his relatives seven years earlier!

The people on this farm were Mr. and Mrs. Skinner, their three children, (Deidre, Saul and Carl), and Mrs. Skinner's sister, Elsie (oh how she loved scandal!). However, Elsie was a very valuable member of the farm-household. Every day, even Sunday, she baked in the oven beside and heated by the fire six large loaves of bread to feed the large, hungry household. Every other day she also made teacakes, the days in between making cakes, biscuits and pastries! The Skinners also employed another farm-worker, Alan, as well as William.

William found, like many other employees have done before and since, that it is only when you are actually employed by someone or living with someone, that you begin to learn their faults. William soon learnt that Mr. Skinner's hygiene was poor. The thought of a farm-worker having frequent baths amused Mr. Skinner and he called William "fancy-man!".

"Has fancy-man had his bath?" Mr. Skinner would ask his wife.

"Aye, he has. And it would dee thee a deal of good if thou had 'un!" his poor wife would reply.

"Bah!" would snort Mr. Skinner. "If one leaves the dirt long enough it will drop off!"

Not many years later, William helped to carry Mrs. Skinner upstairs, dying of cancer. I do not know which form of cancer she had. I wonder if it were cervical cancer. Researchers have found that the wives of blue-collar workers i.e. wives whose husbands have dirty jobs, are more likely to develop this form of cancer than white-collar workers wives. Researchers have also found that poor hygiene on the part of the husband increases the chances of his wife getting cervical cancer. One wonders whether or not Mrs. Skinner's cancer was cervical, and if it were how much blame for it could be placed at her husband's door.

Mr. Skinner's dirty habits did not stop with himself, but were to be seen on the farm as well. Today cows are milked by machines. The milk goes directly from the cow into a covered container. However, before milking machines, the milker sat on a small stool and milked into a bucket. These bucketfuls of milk were then tipped into cans, which did have lids, but which Mr. Skinner often could not be bothered to put on. Cats are always plentiful on a farm (there is work for them keeping the mouse population down!) and they love getting in the milking parlour where the milk is to be found. Cans without lids were great temptations to the cats, and William would often find them balanced precariously on the top of a can trying to lap the milk.

"You should put the lids on the cans to stop the cats getting the milk!" William told Mr. Skinner.

"I thought cats were clean creatures they're always washing themselves!" replied his boss.

"So they are", answered William, "but the tongue they lap the milk with, is the same tongue that licks the cat's backside!"

No wonder governments over the years have had to legislate about hygiene when people behave like this!

The same gentleman would rise from bed and start the morning milking without washing his hands first! William also recalls how even milk with blood in it was not scrapped!

William was popular with Carl and Saul. He bought them "Meccano", that metal construction-set that can be used to make many toys and models. These days, since the invention of plastics, children have many brightly coloured plastic toys. However, toys in days gone by were not so plentiful and were much duller in colour. The new paint on toys very rapidly wore off.

"William," said Carl, "there's a rat in the barn!"

"How do you know?" asked William.

"When I've opened the barn-door I've seen it, but it always runs away somewhere", answered Carl.

William hated rats. However, perhaps to be friendly with Carl he found himself saying,

"Let's go and see if it's there now! We'd better take a torch with us".

The two of them went out of the farm-house, and walked through the farmyard until they came to the barn-door.

"Shhh now!" whispered William to Carl before they entered the outbuilding.

Slowly William opened the barn-door and the two of them crept inside. Carl tapped William's arm and pointed. William's eyes followed the line from Carl's finger. Yes, there he was on the barn-floor, eating some grain which had been spilt.

Almost as soon as William noticed the rat, the rat noticed his observers. It left what it was eating and ran up the wooden supports onto the next floor of the barn. William followed him, not daring to take his eyes off him, lest he vanish again. Luckily, a hay-pin was standing near the wall, William grabbed it, without taking his eyes off the rat. Slowly he ascended the stairs of the barn, torch in one hand, hay-pin in the other. The rat, however, ran up some sacks, up the rough wall, and sat between the top of the wall and the roof, eyeing the ascending William. William stepped off the stairs, and moved slowly over to the wall, chaser and chased watching each other. He was now about eye level with the rat. The rat's bright eyes and glistening front teeth could be seen clearly in the light of the torch. William slowly raised his hay-pin and then brought it crashing down between the eyes of the almost hypnotised rat.

"Got it!"

William's triumphant shout to Carl broke the silence.

William had it up on the end of the hay-pin for Carl to see. The latter had now dashed up the steps and was standing beside him.

"What an aim, William! Look at his size! I'm going to tell Saul about all this!" exclaimed Carl, and he dashed out of the building, leaving William to deal with the rodent.

Mrs. Skinner liked having William on the farm. He grew vegetables in the farm kitchen garden for the family, and bought a stone of eating apples from the owner of a nearby orchard inviting the family to help themselves.

"I wish all men were like you!" Mrs. Skinner used to exclaim, no doubt dwelling on her husband's failings.

"I hear you're going on a trip to Whitby, Deidre", said William.

"That's right", replied Deidre.

"Here's half-a-crown for you to spend there!" went on William, placing a large silver coin in her hand.

"Thanks William", responded Deidre.

Half-a-crown is equivalent to twelve and a half pence now. It was the author's Christmas present from many relatives for many years in the nineteen fifties.

When Deidre returned from Whitby, William noticed her carrying a packet of cigarettes to her father as a present from Whitby. Seeing William she quickly hid them under her apron.

"Are you telling me, that you brought your father something from Whitby and not William who gave you the money?" exclaimed a shocked Mrs. Skinner to Deidre.

"That's the way it is", replied Deidre.

Indeed, that was the way it was. Deidre had no time for William: he was a farm-worker and she wanted to marry a farmer! Nevertheless, she did not think twice about helping herself to his chocolates which he had not given the family permission to eat!

One evening William was sitting drinking in a pub. He became a little uneasy because he felt a man in a corner was watching him. The next minute the man dropped into a seat the other side of William's table.

"I've been watching you for a while", he began. "You wouldn't be William who used to work for old Ingledew, out Northallerton way, would you?"

"Aye, I used to work for him", replied William. "But how do you know me?"

"You just fitted the description I've been given of you. I used to work for him as well. They told me you worked there two years. How you stuck that place two years I'll never know. They're mad on that farm, quite mad! I only stuck it there six months!"

Mr. Skinner did not like his money being spent. When coal or more flour was needed the household was afraid to mention it. More than once when he noticed the family had been to the mill for flour, he did not speak to them for a week!

"You've forgotten to butter the bread, Mrs. Skinner", said William one day at table.

Mr. Skinner was out of the room at that moment. Mrs. Skinner replied,

"Mr. Skinner does not want us to put butter on farm-workers bread!"

"I'll tell you what to do!" smiled William. "You butter the bread, and I'll eat it upside down!"

Once Mr. Skinner allowed a batch of day old chicks to die, because he was either unwilling to spend money on a house for them, or too lazy to be bothered to make one!

"Bah!" grunted Mr. Skinner. "That one won't survive!"

Mr. Skinner was gazing at the two calves Clover, his cow, had just produced. One was a fine specimen of a calf, but the other was small and very weak.

"I think we'll kill this one right away", said Mr. Skinner.

"Oh Mr. Skinner don't!" pleaded William.

"I tell you lad, it's not worth bothering with, it probably won't last the night!"

"Mr. Skinner, could I have that calf? I'll take it to that old damp stable we don't use. It will be out of your sight", went on William.

"I tell you lad, you'll be wasting your time over it", emphasised Skinner.

"Please Mr. Skinner", begged William.

"All right then", relented his boss. "But remember, you've been warned, you're wasting your efforts on it!"

"Thank you", said William edging towards his calf.

Suddenly Mr. Skinner looked worried and altered the tone of his voice.

"Mind you", he began, "if it does pull round, remember the calf belongs to this farm, it's not yours!"

"I understand", said William quickly.

The happy William did what he could to make the damp, old stable as comfortable as possible for his calf. He believed in giving animals plenty of bedding and good food.

"You know, I begin to think old Skinner was right about you", said William stroking his calf. "You won't feed. Perhaps you'll have your milk if I lift it to your face. There's a good calf, have a nice drink".

The days passed and the calf did not die. However, it would only feed if William lifted its food up to its head. It could not get the idea of bending down to get its food.

"Come on Midget", coaxed William. "You've got to put your head down. I can't feed you like this for ever!"

Then William got the idea of slowly lowering the bucket day by day, until at last the calf would take its food in the normal way.

"That's the idea!" exclaimed William when his calf fed properly. "Well I must say you're coming on fine. Just now old Skinner will be wanting you in the herd with your twin sister!"

That, of course, is what happened, and the young calf went on to be one of Mr. Skinner's best milking cows!

"I don't know", puzzled Mr. Skinner one day, "that old ewe had twin lambs, and now there's another running with her! We must have a stray from another farm, but I don't know how!"

"It's that little lamb I told you about", said William. "Don't you remember?"

The story was that one day William had been in the sheep-field and had spotted a very weak lamb in the field. It had been born under some trees and was unable to stand. In such a state it would have died, being unable to keep up with its mother and the other two triplets. William once more had taken it to an outbuilding, given it good bedding and hand fed it, so that soon it was able to skip with its fellows in the Spring sunshine.

––––––––––––––

"That's twenty-five piglets! Did you ever hear of a pig having twenty-five piglets at once?" asked and exclaimed Mr. Skinner at the same time.

Mr. Skinner and William surveyed the sow and all her piglets.

"Of course", said Mr. Skinner, "some of these are bound to die. She can't possible feed all these. So don't you be giving them extra bedding William!"

However, when Mr. Skinner was elsewhere, William used to enter the pig-sty and supply the small piglets with extra straw for warmth. This can be likened to the practice of putting very small babies in incubators to give them warmth. Not one of those piglets died, and William had to confess what he had done when asked directly by Mr. Skinner. However, no doubt with twenty-five pigs to sell or eat Mr. Skinner would not be too harsh with William!

––––––––––––––

"Bah! It's cold out there!" snorted Mr. Skinner, rubbing his hands in front of the fire. "Why's this fire got so little coal on?" questioned the farmer.

"You know why", answered Mrs. Skinner calmly. "We hardly have any left and I'm trying to save it, since I know how little you like spending money on coal!"

"Well we're going to have to have some", said Mr. Skinner firmly. "What a winter! I've never known such bitterly cold temperatures before!" he continued grumbling.

"You can't go with the cart and get coal from the station in this frost, the horses won't be able to grip on the banks!" protested Mrs. Skinner.

"Bah! I'll send William", said Mr. Skinner. "If anyone can manage the horses, he can!"

"Poor William!" exclaimed Mrs. Skinner. "You should have sent him before conditions got as bad as this!"

William set out for the coal. He led the first horse and the other horse was between the wooden shafts pulling the cart.

What a day it was! There was a layer of white frost covering everything: grass, hedges, fences, walls, buildings and the road! One could see one's breath in the cold air! William did not under estimate the danger of his job. He could sense that even his horses were afraid, because they were sweating in spite of the cold morning!

"You've got a job there lad!" shouted some men in sympathy as he passed them.

William tried to get his horses to put one hoof on the grass verge where possible, in order to give them a better grip than they would have on the slippery road.

Finally, he reached the station, bought the coal and set off home, knowing that the return would be worse than the outward journey, because of the heavy load the horses had to pull up the slippery hills and hold back on the descents.

Back on the farm, Mr. Skinner thought about William and softened a little. Yes, he had set him a hard job in view of the appalling conditions. And so, the rather lazy farmer, who rode on horseback round his farm rather than walk, set off to meet William, with an extra horse for him!

———————

"There's a farm for sale", announced Mr. Skinner to William one day. "I'd like you and Chris to go and have a look at it for me. You know what to look for!"

It seems strange to me that a farmer would send his farm-labourer to look at a farm prior to purchase. However, that is what happened. William and Chris paid a visit to the farm and then reported back to Mr. Skinner.

"Well, what did you think of the farm then?" asked his boss on their return.

"It's a good farm, Mr. Skinner", replied William. "There's only one thing wrong with it!"

"Oh, what's that?" inquired the farmer.

"It's too far to the nearest pub for you!" quipped William.

"Oh we won't bother with it then!" laughed Skinner.

Then came the time when Mr. Skinner fell ill.

"Whatever are we going to do if anything happens to your husband?" asked Elsie.

"William will have to run the farm for us", answered Mrs. Skinner calmly.

William pricked up his ears. Was he really going to manage this farm? For a time he and Alan kept the farm running. Then Mr. Skinner recovered, took the reins himself again, and so once more farm management eluded William.

The years rolled by. One day, William was working in a field, when he noticed some men working near a bridge.

"I know one of those men", William mused, "but it can't be so far from home. It must be his double", he went on. "And yet, I'm sure it is my step-father. Now, if it is, am I going to stand my ground or get out of sight?"

While William was pondering these things, he himself was spotted.

"I don't believe it! Is it William?" asked one of the group of men pausing from his work.

William nodded and recognised his step-father even though many years had elapsed.

"So, this is where you ran to!" exclaimed the older man.

"Oh no!' corrected William. "I've worked on other farms before this one!"

"Are you married?" asked his father.

"No," replied William, "but I've had a few girl-friends over the years".

"I see. By, it's a hot day. One gets dry working outside", said the older man changing the subject.

"Come along to the farmhouse and I'll see if I can get you fixed up with a cup of tea or something", invited William.

"Well, that's very kind of you lad", said his father. "You lead the way".

William led the older man over the fields. They had to walk in single file as they moved between hedge and a field of swaying golden wheat, bespattered here and there with bright red poppies.

At length they came to open pasture where young bullocks were grazing. They looked up as the men passed, and then returned to the business of feeding. Now that they were side by side again, it was William's turn to ask a question.

"What were you doing near that bridge?"

"I've got a job with a firm and we are testing the foundations of that bridge", his step-father replied.

"I see", said William.

"When are you coming home lad?" his step-father said suddenly. "Your ma often talks about you!"

"Does she now!" replied William, not answering the question.

Later that evening, when the men had gone, William found himself meditating on his step-father's words.

"When are you coming home lad? Your ma often talks about you", ran through his head.

"No, I'm not going home. I'm not even going to visit her. She's not worth the bus-fare", thought William.

Indeed, so badly had Sybil treated William, that the intervening years had not eased William's painful remembrance of her! Furthermore, logic tells William that his mother is dead now, but he neither knows when she died, nor where she is buried!

"I've got a man, Adam, coming to thatch some straw stacks for us today", announced Mr. Skinner.

This announcement rather upset William. He regarded himself as a good, all-round farm-man and perfectly capable of thatching any kind of stack. Indeed, his thatching had been praised by a certain squire before that day. Somehow William felt that Adam was being employed in order to frustrate him! Mr. Skinner should have been pleased that he had employed William in 1928, and had kept him on over the years, but William's ability seemed to breed in his employer jealousy rather than satisfaction or gratitude.

"There's nowt so queer as folks!" is a frequent expression of William's, and very applicable here.

William was not the only person to notice Mr. Skinner's lack of gratitude.

"Tell Skinner I turned a sheep over for him the other day", asked a local keeper of William one evening.

Now a sheep left on its back will die if no one rights it, because the thin legs of a sheep are unable to turn its heavy woolly body over! However, instead of Mr. Skinner being pleased with the keeper for saving his sheep (and his money!) he could only grunt when William passed on the message,

"That's nothing!"

Winter came and the straw in Adam's straw-stacks had to be used. A stack is a way of keeping various grasses. The thatch on the top ensures the contents keep dry, that is if it is done properly!

"And don't give those beasts any more damp bedding!" Skinner snapped at William.

"And where am I to get dry straw from?" quipped William angrily.

Mr. Skinner could not answer this. Adam had let Mr. Skinner down badly in that his thatching did not keep the rain out of the stacks!

It is said that you can be too long in one place. I think William was at Mr. Skinner's. Even the relationship between Skinner's sons and William seemed to be turning sour! Once William found them kicking his seedlings in the vegetable garden he looked after for the farm. Anyone who has ever managed to get seeds to germinate will know how heart-breaking that must have been!

"Let's get him!" Saul whispered to Carl that say.

William happened to overhear him. Forgotten now were all memories of how William had bought them Meccano out of his small wage! One might have thought that two, healthy country-born young men, now in their teens, would have been able to cause William considerable injury very quickly. However, I am glad to say that that was not the case. William was not tall but was stocky and had a lot of strength in his muscles. William rapidly managed to overpower them both! (Remember the seventeen stone of maize William carried at Mr. Ingledew's?).

But just as the fight between Moses and the Egyptian had been witnessed, so a pair of eyes were watching the fight on the farm!

"I was surprised to see you fighting, William!" chirped Elsie, when William had regained his breath and reached the farmhouse!

"You don't miss much, do you Elsie?" replied William.

"I've told my sister", went on Elsie, "and you are to go up and see her immediately".

When William had regained his composure he tiptoed upstairs to dear Mrs. Skinner. Mrs. Skinner was now confined to bed dying of cancer. Indeed, William had helped to carry her there! He explained what had happened to the farmer's wife.

"He's a bad little beggar, Saul", the sick woman managed to utter. "He's just like his father!"

Mrs. Skinner was silent. The poor woman was no doubt reflecting on having brought such an ill-natured child into the world.

When hiring time came round again, Mr. Skinner decided that this time he would not re-employ William, because he now had two sons old enough to help him run the farm. This was 1937, and William was about thirty-two. He had been at Mr. Skinner's nine years.

CONCLUSION

At this point my book should end, because I have recorded William's farming tales as I set out to do. However, those of you who have followed his progress through these pages, will want, I am sure, to know what he did after leaving Mr. Skinner's. So, I will cram about sixty years into a few pages.

William had decided that, "there was no money in farming", that is, as a farm-man. Indeed, on one occasion Mr. Skinner had said he could not afford to pay William his pound a week, but only fifteen shillings (seventy-five new pence). I understand farm-labourers still have low wages.

William therefore made his way, if not to the "big smoke" of London, to the smoke of the industrial towns around the banks of the River Tees. He managed to get a job with the Imperial Chemical Industries (I.C.I.). It would not be unreasonable to ask what skills William had that a chemical industry could want. The I.C.I. has many buildings spread over a large area. William was employed (amongst other things) to cut the grass between these buildings. For larger areas he used a cutter drawn by a horse. For smaller and more awkward areas he used a scythe which could be described as a long curved blade on the end of a long handle.

William was the perfect man for the job. Sometimes there are odd noises in industry. Once there was a dreadful hiss of steam as steam at high pressure was released! William's horse was startled and started to bolt. Down a grassy bank charged the horse, once more with William in tow! (Remember the incident at Mr. Ingledew's years earlier?) Horror came over William as a railway-line at the foot of the bank came into view! It was not a national railway-line, but a works internal goods line. Nevertheless, regardless of who owned the railway, a dreadful accident could have taken place. However, once more, William's skill as a horseman saved the day, and the animal was brought under control before any accident happened.

Joining the I.C.I. around the time the Second World War started, (1939), William received his twenty-year service watch in 1959, his thirty-year watch in 1969, and finally retired in 1970 at the age of sixty-five. During this time he enjoyed very good health.

While William was with Mr. Skinner it had been a very barren time as far as affairs of the heart were concerned. William simply did not meet any desirable and willing young ladies! Do bear in mind that pre-war, people had fewer holidays away from work, only a tiny minority owned motor-cars and men could be on farms day in, day out miles from people in villages and towns.

However, things began to change in this area for William as the Second World War wore on. One day, he was cycling in the country (I believe he was visiting Mr. Skinner!) when he got a flat tyre and had to deal with it. A young lady also cycling in the country (I believe visiting an aunt) overtook him at this point. When William had dealt with his tyre, he mounted his cycle and soon overtook the young woman, only to have to deal with his tyre again further up the road! The young woman was, not surprisingly, a little suspicious of these punctures when she passed him a second time! Apparently this alternate overtaking was repeated several times, until finally the young lady asked if she could be of any assistance!

I will not go into any more details. Let it suffice to say that in October 1944 William and the lady cyclist were married. In 1994 they celebrated their Golden Wedding.

William and his wife (three years his junior) had two daughters (who became teachers) and in turn five grandchildren. You can imagine that he is proud of them all.

Now that William had an industrial wage, he had a little more money. This factor, together with Pearl having encouraged him to save in a building society, enabled him to buy a semi-detached home.

With the example of a greedy mother before him, and having had what little he earned taken from him, one might have expected William to have clung onto all that came his way. Instead, however, he was generous with money and garden produce, to family and work-mates alike! When Joe and Jane needed some cash for a particular purpose, he was able to help them, as they had helped him in his early years.

Perhaps one ought to mention faith before this book closes, since millions would say that it is a very important part of their lives.

After attendance at church and chapel in his early life, William did not attend a place of worship for many years. William seemed pleased with himself for achieving so much after running away from home with virtually nothing. He was self-satisfied; he had done it, God had had no part in it. Indeed, I have even heard him say that he thought God had been dreamed up by the bosses to keep workers in their place! However, I am very happy to say that towards the end of William's life, his faith began to return.

There is, however, one dream of William's that remains, and now will have to remain, unfulfilled. This dream was to own a smallholding, i.e. a very small farm. For various reasons William did not make this pipe-dream a reality. Instead, he had to content himself with caring for his own garden and gardening for many other people who sought his help. One can finish by saying that William's deep love of the country and all living things has been passed onto his children and even grandchildren.

William died whilst this book was being written, only months from his ninetieth birthday.

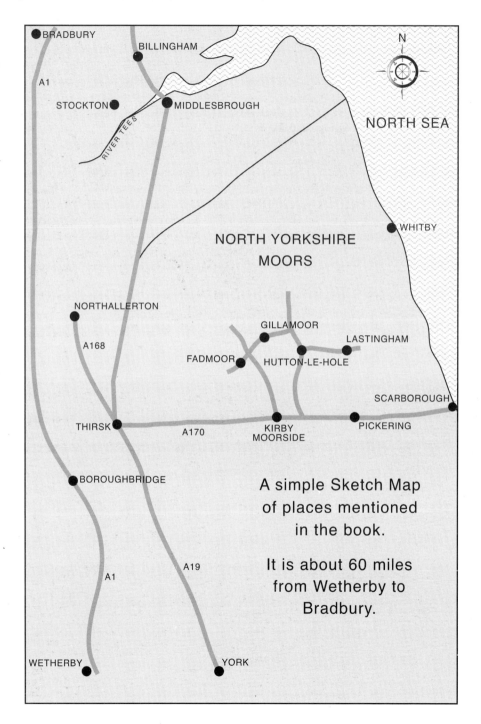

BRADBURY

BILLINGHAM

A1

STOCKTON

MIDDLESBROUGH

RIVER TEES

N

NORTH SEA

WHITBY

NORTH YORKSHIRE
MOORS

NORTHALLERTON

A168

GILLAMOOR

LASTINGHAM

FADMOOR

HUTTON-LE-HOLE

SCARBOROUGH

THIRSK

A170

KIRBY
MOORSIDE

PICKERING

BOROUGHBRIDGE

A simple Sketch Map
of places mentioned
in the book.

It is about 60 miles
from Wetherby to
Bradbury.

A1

A19

WETHERBY

YORK